SCHOLASTIC News

Nonfiction Readers

Math at the Store

by Ellen Weiss

Children's Press®
A Division of Scholastic Inc.
New York Toronto London Auckland Sydney
Mexico City New Delhi Hong Kong
Danbury, Connecticut

These content vocabulary word builders are for grades 1–2.

Math Consultant: Linda K. Voges, EdD, Cohort Coordinator/Lecturer, College of Education, The University of Texas at Austin

Reading Consultant: Cecilia Minden-Cupp, PhD, Early Literacy Consultant and Author, Chapel Hill, North Carolina

Photographs © 2008: Alamy Images/Enigma: 17; Corbis Images/Brian Hagiwara/Brand X: 2, 4 top right; Digital Light Source/Hutchings Stock Photography: 4 bottom left, 5 bottom right, 5 bottom left, 5 top right, 11 bottom, 11 top, 13, 15, 19; PhotoEdit: 5 top left, 21 bottom (Bill Aron), 1, 4 bottom right, 7 (Annette Coolidge), 21 top (Lon C. Diehl), back cover, 9 (Dennis Mac Donald), cover (David Young-Wolff).

Book Design: Simonsays Design!; Book Production: The Design Lab

Library of Congress Cataloging-in-Publication Data

Weiss, Ellen, 1949-
Math at the Store / by Ellen Weiss.
p. cm.—(Scholastic news nonfiction reader)
Includes bibliographical references and index.
ISBN-13: 978-0-531-18528-5 (lib. bdg.) 978-0-531-18781-4 (pbk.)
ISBN-10: 0-531-18528-1 (lib. bdg.) 0-531-18781-0 (pbk.)
1. Mathematics—Juvenile literature. 2. Grocery shopping Mathematics—Juvenile literature.
I. Title. II. Series.
QA40.5.W454 2008
510—dc22   2007000971

CONTENTS

WORD HUNT

Look for these words as you read. They will be in **bold**.

cent
(sent)

gallon
(**gal**-uhn)

prices
(**pri**-sez)

4

dime
(dime)

dozen
(**duhz**-uhn)

quart
(kwort)

stack
(stak)

Math at the Store

This trip to the supermarket is going to be fun.

We need to buy lots of food.

Math helps everyone shop at the store.

Can you read the **prices** on these signs?

2 for $3

2 for $5

deli

LEMONS
5 for $1

RUBY RED GRAPEFRUIT
2 for $1

TEXAS ORANGES
3-99¢

58¢
5-$1
3-99

7

The store has lots of fruit for sale.

Yum, those oranges look good!

Let's buy some.

How many should we buy?

We need 1 **dozen** oranges.

One dozen is another way to say 12.

We already have 8 oranges.

How many more do we need?

Turn to page 23 for the answer.

$$8 + 4 = 12$$

Now we have a dozen oranges!

Look at this **stack** of cans.

The bottom row has 7 cans.

The next row has 6 cans.

Each row has 1 less can than the row below it.

The storekeeper worked hard to stack these cans.

13

Now the storekeeper is building another stack.

Look carefully at this stack.

How many cans should he put on the next row?

Use math to help him find the answer.

Turn to page 23 for the answer.

The highest row
has 4 cans.

We need to buy some milk.

The smaller container is
1 **quart**.

The bigger container is
1 **gallon**.

quarts

gallons

$ 2.59

$ 2.59

$ 3.99

2%

17

There are 4 quarts in 1 gallon.

We need 2 gallons of milk.

How many quarts would that be?

Turn to page 23 for the answer.

quarts

gallon

4 quarts = 1 gallon

One penny equals 1 **cent**.
One **dime** equals 10 cents.

We have 8 dimes.

This juice box costs 75 cents.

Do we have enough money to buy the juice box?

I hope so! We need a treat after so much shopping.

Turn to page 23 for the answer.

YOUR NEW WORDS

cent (sent) unit of money; penny

dime (dime) a small coin worth ten cents

dozen (**duhz**-uhn) twelve of something

gallon (**gal**-uhn) an amount equal to four quarts

prices (**pri**-sez) the amounts that you have to pay for things

quart (kwort) an amount equal to four cups

stack (stak) a pile of items arranged neatly in layers

Page 10

We have 8 oranges. We need 1 dozen, or 12.

$8 + 4 = 12$

We need 4 more oranges.

Page 14

Each row has 1 less can than the row below it.

$4 - 1 = 3$

Page 18

1 gallon = 4 quarts

2 gallons = 4 quarts + 4 quarts

$4 + 4 = 8$

You could also use this number sentence: $4 \times 2 = 8$

Page 20

1 dime = 10¢

8 dimes = 8 x 10¢. That makes 80¢.

80¢ is more than 75¢.

You can buy your treat!

INDEX

FIND OUT MORE

Book:
Roberson, Erin. *All About Money*. New York: Children's Press, 2004.

Website:
FunBrain.com Change Maker
www.funbrain.com/cashreg/index.html

MEET THE AUTHOR

Ellen Weiss has received many awards for her books for kids. She lived in England for a short time where they call the subject "maths."